D1710281

HYPOTHESIS, THEORY, LAW

Shirley Duke

Educational Media

rourkeeducationalmedia.com

Before Reading:

Building Academic Vocabulary and Background Knowledge

Before reading a book, it is important to tap into what your child or students already know about the topic. This will help them develop their vocabulary, increase their reading comprehension, and make connections across the curriculum.

1. *Look at the cover of the book. What will this book be about?*
2. *What do you already know about the topic?*
3. *Let's study the Table of Contents. What will you learn about in the book's chapters?*
4. *What would you like to learn about this topic? Do you think you might learn about it from this book? Why or why not?*
5. *Use a reading journal to write about your knowledge of this topic. Record what you already know about the topic and what you hope to learn about the topic.*
6. *Read the book.*
7. *In your reading journal, record what you learned about the topic and your response to the book.*
8. *After reading the book complete the activities below.*

Content Area Vocabulary
Read the list. What do these words mean?
controversy
data
equation
fact
falsifiable
hypothesis
inferences
law
logical
model
outcome
paradigm
peer review
scientific inquiry
scientific method

After Reading:

Comprehension and Extension Activity

After reading the book, work on the following questions with your child or students in order to check their level of reading comprehension and content mastery.

1. *When is the data and knowledge from experiments finally accepted? (Summarize)*
2. *How does controversy further science? (Asking questions)*
3. *Why are peer reviews needed in science? (Asking questions)*
4. *What is the purpose of a hypothesis? (Summarize)*
5. *How do scientific experiments effect our lives? (Text to self connection)*

Extension Activity

Observe your classroom. What seems to make students work better? Create your own "if-then" statement, or hypothesis, and share it with a classmate. Continue to develop your hypothesis by collecting data through experiments. Record your experiments and observations exactly. Write a report on your findings and have your classmate conduct the same experiment. Did he or she get the same results as you? Was anything different between the two experiments?

Table of Contents

CHAPTER ONE

What Is Science Inquiry?

Most people have probably heard the story about Isaac Newton sitting under an apple tree. One day, an apple fell on his head, and he discovered the law of gravity. But, it didn't really happen that way!

The falling apple made Newton think about why the apple fell in the first place. What was it that brought the apple to the ground? A series of questions unfolded. As Newton answered his own questions, he saw that a force acted on the apple. That force was gravity.

Sir Isaac Newton (1643–1727)

Newton arrived at the idea of gravity in a way similar to how scientists work today. **Scientific inquiry** is the way scientists study the natural world. As they explore, they develop explanations based on what they learn from their work.

Scientists explore the unknown to understand their world through scientific inquiry. They investigate and provide explanations for what they find.

Most new discoveries don't fall into someone's lap, or on their head. Scientists follow a specific process that helps them make scientific discoveries. Scientists make observations and ask questions. They make a **hypothesis** based on what they have seen. They conduct experiments to learn more.

Over time, when many experiments have shown the same results, this body of knowledge becomes accepted. Now, it's a scientific theory.

A scientific theory is built on layers of knowledge and many tests. Sound reasoning supports the many facts. It's nowhere near a guess!

Scientific law makes a statement about a general rule. A law happens every time and never varies. Scientific laws explain things. Yet, they don't describe them. A law can predict what will happen, but it does not tell why.

Science cannot give 100 percent proof to ideas. It states facts from direct observations. At a later time, new facts may arise that change the laws. The new information is added and the law is adjusted.

Mapping out the steps for an investigation is another part of scientific inquiry. Collecting information follows. Then ideas are adjusted as the work continues. Scientists record evidence, measure, and observe. Next, they communicate what was learned.

Scientific inquiry takes any scientist at any age from simple ideas to more complex ideas. The process helps to form a body of knowledge. It moves from a hypothesis to a theory and maybe even to a law. Everyone who works in science follows the same process, and it often proves to be exciting.

CHAPTER TWO

From Fact to Knowledge

A scientific **fact** is learned by direct observation. You see it happen or experience it. Birds fly. That's a fact because you have seen it with your eyes. But, when you say the Sun will rise tomorrow, you have not stated a fact. Of course, it is very likely going to happen, but you haven't seen it so far! Reports of something happening or using past information are helpful to predict future behavior, but not considered facts in science.

Repeated observations lead to **inferences**. Reports from trusted scientists or historians can be very useful in making inferences. Some inferences are conclusions based on solid reasoning from now-accepted ideas. Others come from repeated observations.

If you were to roll a toy car down a ramp from a starting line, the results will let you infer what will happen if you repeat the process. But, it won't be a fact until you actually let it roll.

A hypothesis is an idea you can test to explain something that happens. Often a hypothesis will direct you to more facts. The testing of a hypothesis is important. A good hypothesis is designed to be tested. However, a problem comes if a factor that cannot be tested is added.

Hypothesis: The heat from the Sun will melt this ice.

A hypothesis that is wrong is as helpful as one that is right.

A theory comes from a group of like ideas that explain happenings and are based on facts. Scientists use this information to predict observations to come. Creating a theory takes place after a long period of testing.

Much of science is based on theories. The theory of gravity lets someone know not to walk over the edge of a cliff. Astronauts fly into space and return based on the theory of gravity.

Evidence is found in direct observations and measurements. Theories are not evidence. But evidence does support theories. Scientists check their work by asking what they know and why they know it.

Results: The hypothesis is found to be correct.

A **paradigm** is a typical pattern for a way of thinking. If all scientists are looking at the world in the same way, based on a false assumption, they may not be seeing the truth.

Continental Drift Theory

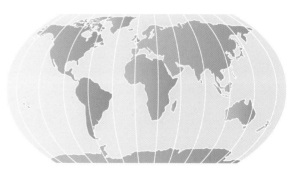

For years people believed the Earth's crust didn't move. Later, people thought it was possible that the continents had "drifted," moving through the oceans.

Changing a paradigm means changing the focus of an idea. Often, scientists aren't aware that they are interpreting their observations according to a false paradigm.

However, as new **data** are discovered, scientific knowledge grows. Good scientific practices support new learning.

Tectonic Plate Theory

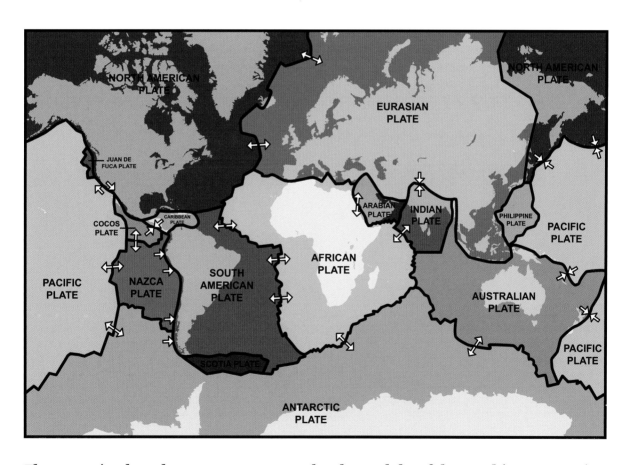

The tectonic plate theory now suggests that huge slabs of the Earth's crust are in constant motion, driven by the heat inside the Earth's core.

CHAPTER THREE

Developing a Hypothesis

Many students learn the definition of a hypothesis in the early grades. It is often defined as an educated guess. But a hypothesis includes far more information than a simple guess. A hypothesis is a well-constructed statement based on information. The scientist designs the test to learn more or prove it right or wrong.

A hypothesis serves as a building block for learning new information. The experiments that follow a hypothesis may also lead to more proof of something already known.

If I do (this) _ _ _ _ _ then (this) _ _ _ _ _ will happen.

A scientist forms a hypothesis based on experience and data. The scientist is well studied in the topic. Multiple, early observations form the basis of a hypothesis.

A good hypothesis leads the researcher to new facts about a topic. Remember, facts are made of information that has been observed. They are known to be true. The hypothesis seeks facts, but the **outcome** will not be known until the experiment is complete. The researcher knows what results he or she expects to see. However, the results may turn out to be far different from what was expected. But that is not a bad thing. Either way, the scientist has learned something new.

A hypothesis must be **logical**. A logical hypothesis is based on valid thinking and quality reasoning.

A good hypothesis is also **falsifiable**. This means the wording is stated so that the hypothesis can also be proven incorrect if there are data to show that. A hypothesis contains no right or wrong answer. There is only the answer that comes from evidence.

An illogical hypothesis might include a condition that cannot be tested. A hypothesis that depends on Bigfoot showing up is not a logical hypothesis.

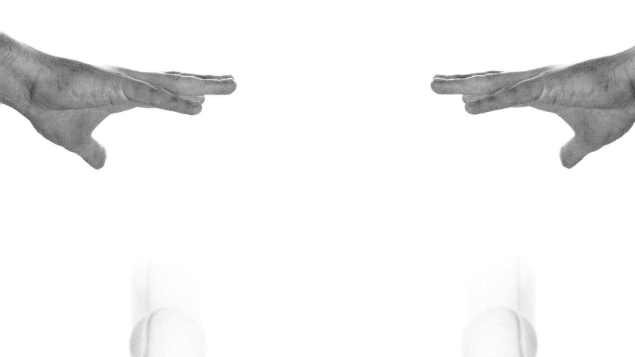

Hypothesis: The ball will bounce higher on the grass than on the sidewalk (or vice versa).

Sidewalk	Grass

The scientist will then test the idea stated in the hypothesis. This test must be designed as an experiment that will give a result. The researcher will use prior knowledge to design the experiment.

Researchers must accept the results of the test. They can't ignore data that goes against the hypothesis if it turns up. This "cherry-picking" method of choosing only the results that support the hypothesis is not real science.

Other scientists must be able to test the hypothesis as well. Repeated testing by other scientists tests for errors and wrong data. This is a **peer review**.

Some journals will not publish a scientist's study until it has gone through peer review.

If other scientists get the same results in repeated tests, the information can be confirmed as true. If the test often gives different results, the hypothesis must be adjusted or changed. As more and more facts are learned, the hypothesis may point to a theory.

CHAPTER FOUR

What's a Theory?

A scientific theory is a broad explanation about the natural world backed up by facts. It is presented as a **model** or explanation. Scientists use observations, experiments, and reasoning to explain their theory. Their information has been tested and retested. Others agree on the findings. Theories serve as a foundation for science knowledge.

Studying Tornadoes

Step 1: Observe

Step 2: Experiment

Tornado/Microburst
Simulator

IOWA STATE UNIVERSITY

A theory includes facts that can be directly observed. It comes after many hypotheses have been tested and repeated by others. Scientists use information learned from many hypotheses to describe a scientific theory.

Step 3: Experiment Repeated

Step 4: Explain

Scientists may disagree on a scientific theory. Yet, the basic facts do not change. What they disagree on is how those facts are interpreted, and what they mean for science.

Buoyancy

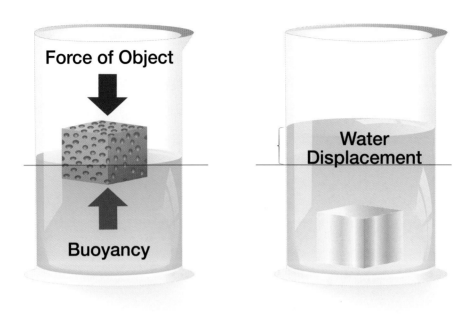

Buoyancy is how well something floats or sinks. If the weight of the object is lighter than the amount of water displaced, it will float, like the sponge. If the object is heavier than the water it moves, the object will sink, like the piece of metal.

A theory is thought to be valid as long as there is no evidence that goes against it. However, new information may turn up. Like hypotheses, theories can be rejected if new facts are discovered that go against the idea. On the other hand, theories can be improved or changed if new information is learned to make them more accurate.

Accepted theories give the best explanation of observable science. They have been tested, contain multiple kinds of evidence, and provide explanations. Yet, some theories may have some problems. Small parts may not fit the observations exactly.

Scientists study the parts that don't fit. They may discover a way in which that part does support the theory. Or their research may also lead to a new theory. Over time, pieces are filled in.

Gaia Theory

The Gaia theory suggests that the Earth and its living and nonliving factors evolved together and work together to maintain its balance, even through changing conditions.

Isaac Newton's laws of **mechanics** were widely accepted. Mechanics is the branch of mathematics working with forces and motion caused by forces. Newton stated three laws of motion. These laws explained forces and motion based on the current knowledge.

Newton's Three Laws of Motion

First Law: A body at rest will tend to stay at rest and a body in motion will stay in motion unless other forces act on it.

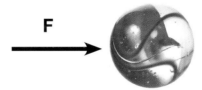

Second Law: Force = Mass × Acceleration (F = MA).

Third Law: For every action there is an equal and opposite reaction.

Discoveries Through the Years

1200s

Robert Grosseteste develops the framework for science experimenting.

1500s

Copernicus states the model in which Earth and planets revolve around the Sun.

1700s

- *Benjamin Franklin discovers lightning is electrical.*
- *Antoine Lavoisier finds law of conservation of mass.*

1900s

- *Albert Einstein explains his theories of relativity.*
- *Jonas Salk creates the polio vaccine.*
- *James D. Watson and Francis Crick identify the structure of DNA.*

2000s

The human genome is mapped.

1400s

Leonardo da Vinci uses notebooks to collect evidence on the body, optics, and water.

1600s

- *Johannes Kepler states laws of planetary motion.*
- *Galileo Galilei improves the telescope and studies the Sun and planets.*
- *Isaac Newton explains his laws of motion.*

1800s

- *Alessandro Volta defines properties of chemistry and electricity and made a battery.*
- *John Dalton defines atomic theory, which states that all matter is made of atoms.*
- *Gregor Mendel explains laws of inheritance in genetics.*
- *Wilhelm Conrad Roentgen discovers X-rays.*
- *George Ohm provides scientists with the basis for understanding how to control electrical charges.*

27

Later, Albert Einstein predicted differences in motion with his theory of special relativity. Einstein's work showed that Newton's laws were correct, but they changed when speeds neared the speed of light. He also showed that gravity breaks down in extremely strong gravity fields, like around black holes.

Einstein's theory of special relativity linked space and time. The universe can be seen as having three space dimensions (up/down, left/right, forward/ backward) and one time dimension.

Albert Einstein's theory stated that $E = mc^2$, energy equals mass multiplied by the speed of light squared. He received a Nobel Prize for his work in physics in 1921.

Changes in theory sometimes bring about **controversy**. Scientists disagree on data interpretation or what ideas must be studied further. The results move science forward.

Charles Darwin's theory of evolution set off a huge controversy. People grew outraged at the ideas in his book. He stated that evolution takes place through natural selection. He also explained how common ancestors give rise to different species. People believed he was going against the church.

Even today, some people do not accept Darwin's theory of evolution. However, the theory offers a strong scientific idea that unifies all the ideas of biology.

Charles Darwin (1809–1882)

Theory of Evolution

According to the theory of evolution, humans may have evolved from an ape-like animal that lived thousands of years ago.

Big Bang Theory

13.8 Billion Years Ago
Big Bang.

First Seconds After Big Bang
Birth of subatomic particles, including mesons, neutrinos, and quarks.

380,000 Years Later
Electrons and nuclei combined into atoms.

300 Million Years Later
Beginning formation of the stars and galaxies.

9 Billion Years Later
Formation of the solar system and Earth.

Expanding and Cooling Universe

The universe was once compressed into a tiny space until a great force started causing it to expand. The universe is still expanding today.

31

Accepted theories offer the best scientific explanation for the ways the world works. A solid theory has been tested. It is supported by multiple sets of evidence, and has been useful for explaining the natural world. It leads to even more science exploration.

A theory is more certain than a hypothesis. However, it is not as definite as a scientific law.

The Doppler Effect

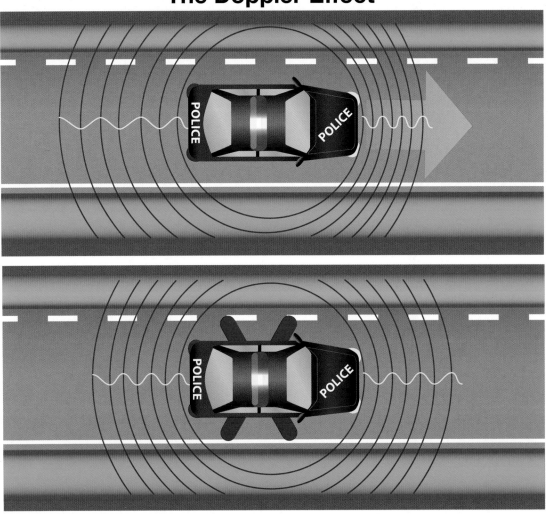

The Doppler effect makes sounds seem to change when the source of the sound or the person listening are moving by compacting the sound waves in front and as the sound passes, the sound waves spread out. A police car sounds higher when it is coming toward you (the sound is moving closer) and makes a lower sound as it passes you (the sound is getting further away), so there is a change in pitch of the sound.

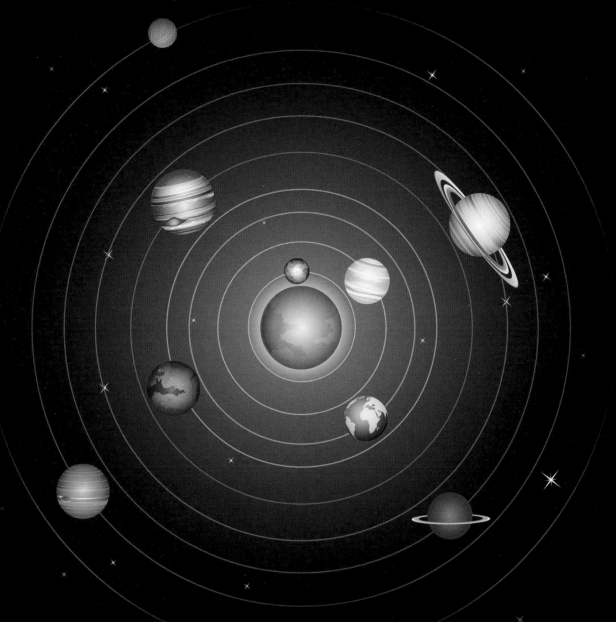

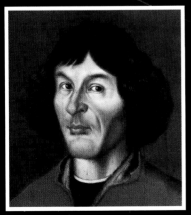

**Nicolaus Copernicus
(1473–1543)**

Did You Know?

Copernicus wrote about his idea that the Sun was the center of the universe in 1514. Until then, people believed the Sun and everything else orbited the Earth. Still, he waited 39 years to publish his idea. He kept quiet because he knew his idea would upset the Church. Making the Sun the center made Earth seem less important. Copernicus's heliocentric model was ridiculed. It took over 50 years for scientists to accept his ideas, as seen in the model diagram above.

CHAPTER FIVE

Scientific Laws

A theory explains observations. On occasion, it becomes a law. However, a theory stands on its own. It explains how nature works.

A scientific law, on the other hand, describes what nature does under a set of conditions. It predicts what will happen if those conditions are in place. Some scientists define scientific law using equations.

More laws exist in physics and chemistry than biology. It is easier to relate physics and chemistry as math expressions. But life science does not typically fit as well in a math **equation**.

Let's Review

Laws	have a tested and proven hypothesis.
	are supported by large amounts of data.
	are accepted by most of the scientists in their fields.
Theories	bring together related ideas in a field of science.
	can be proven incorrect with new data.

Questioning theories and laws strengthens their science. It leads to more scientific inquiry. All scientists ask questions. When no exceptions are found to a theory, it may become a law.

Laws are statements of principle. They are always true and have no known exceptions. Scientific laws are based on a large amount of data and observations.

Most scientists work and question within their own field of science. A biologist, for example, likely hasn't been trained enough to critique the theory of relativity in physics.

Did You Know?

Gregor Mendel tested pea plants by crossing them to grow offspring. By changing one trait at a time, he noticed repeating patterns in the generations. His work led to the laws of heredity.

Gregor Mendel 1822–1884

Newton's law of gravity is one example of a law. This law can predict gravity. However it doesn't explain why gravity exists. The law generalizes information like knowing that if a ball or apple drops from a height, it will fall down and not up. People trust that they will remain firmly on Earth and not go flying into space with each step.

Another example of scientific laws are Kepler's laws of planetary motion. They describe the motions of the planets. However, the laws do not offer an explanation for them.

Scientific laws are far less common than theories. As a law takes shape, each idea is explored through the **scientific method**.

Kepler's Laws of Planetary Motion

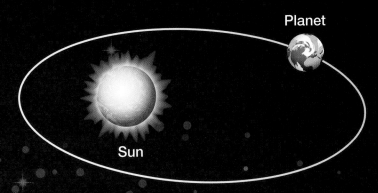

First Law   *Planets move in an elliptical orbit so that the Sun isn't in the exact center of a circle but in a space inside the oval.*

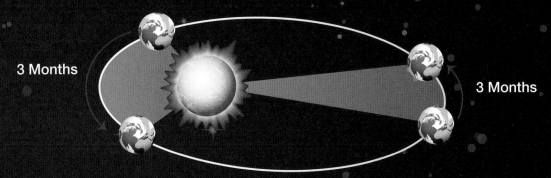

Second Law   *The speed that a planet orbits varies in its position to the Sun while still remaining in a balanced pattern.*

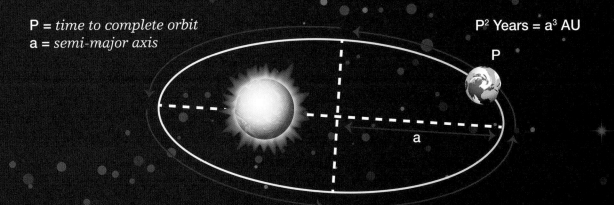

Third Law   *The amount of time a planet takes to go around the Sun can be calculated to show that the farther away a planet is from the Sun, the longer it will take to go around it once.*

CHAPTER SIX

The Scientific Method at Work

The scientific method defines the steps scientists take to explain the natural events of the universe. It makes use of a logical system to study, analyze, and test discoveries. Yet, science is not carried out in a clear, straight line. Science is exciting, repeatable, and spreads in all directions.

The Scientific Method

PURPOSE
State the problem

RESEARCH
Find out about the topic

HYPOTHESIS
State the expected outcome

EXPERIMENT
Develop a procedure to test the hypothesis

ANALYZE
Record the results of the experiment

CONCLUSION
Compare the hypothesis to the experiment's conclusion

40

Scientists begin by asking questions. They research all they can about their question. They learn new information that may lead to more questions. If a scientist has a question that he or she cannot find an answer to, it may be a good question to investigate through an experiment.

The next step is to look for patterns. Then scientists form a hypothesis to explain an observation they have made repeatedly. They create a test that will supply them with quality research data.

Analyzing data shows the results. The conclusion states what was learned. It also reflects the accuracy of the hypothesis. The research and results are accepted and published. They are now available for peer review.

Most fields in science publish professional journals like *Nature* or *Scientific American*. New ideas and research information are reported in these journals. Scientists in the field can read about the findings and test them. Some scientists might interpret the same data differently. Those who oppose the idea carry out their own tests to try and prove the new idea wrong. Sometimes the debates get fierce.

One theory that started a strong debate tried to explain the dinosaur extinction. The Alvarez Impact Theory stated a 6-mile-wide (9.66-kilometer) meteorite hit the Earth 65 million years ago. As a result of the hit, the dinosaurs died out. Even though this theory was proposed in 1979, it took ten years for most scientists to agree.

Luis Alvarez (1911–1988)
Walter Alvarez (1940–)

Did You Know?

When the idea and data stand after all debates, it becomes a theory. It might be changed a bit or rejected later if new facts are learned. A theory is open to arguments as new evidence comes in.

The rare theories that stand up to debates over time may become a law. Newton's law of gravity survives today, even though some adjustments came from Einstein's theory.

The scientific method has limits. What happened before Earth formed can't be studied by observation. Science explains how something works, but not its purpose. It doesn't tell why. It can't be known without observations.

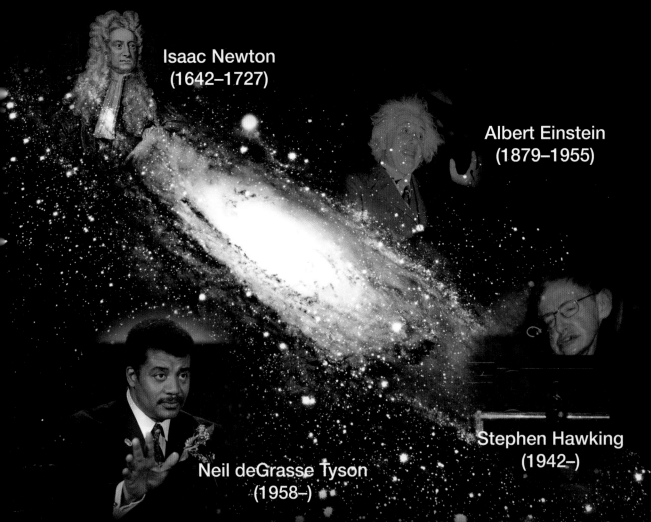

Isaac Newton
(1642–1727)

Albert Einstein
(1879–1955)

Stephen Hawking
(1942–)

Neil deGrasse Tyson
(1958–)

The universe is filled with dark matter. Scientists don't know what it's made of, although they've known about it for 80 years. Scientists who study the stars and universe know it's a big part of the universe. The answer to the mystery of dark matter may be just around the corner.

Try This!

Write Your Science Fair Hypothesis

1. Think about what topic of science you like.

2. Choose three to five books about that topic.

3. Read those books and then narrow down an idea.

4. Narrow your topic.

5. Ask a question about the topic.

6. Now write your hypothesis:

   Tell what you think will happen if you _____.

7. Share your hypothesis with your family and teacher.

Time to experiment!

Glossary

controversy (kahn-truh-VUR-see): a prolonged disagreement over two sides of an idea

data (DAY-tuh): collected facts or observed or measured sets of information

equation (i-KWAY-zhuhn): a mathematical statement of equality

fact (FAKT): a proven and true piece of information

falsifiable (fawl-suh-FYE-uh-buhl): being able to prove that something is not correct

hypothesis (hye-PAH-thi-sis): a reasonable explanation or answer to a scientific question to be tested and that will be proven correct or incorrect

inferences (IN-fur-uhns-is): conclusions drawn after considering all the facts

logical (LAH-ji-kuhl): good, valid reasoning or thought process

model (MAH-duhl): a representation of a set of complex theories or hypotheses that shows a standard for comparing the information

outcome (OUT-kuhm): the result of an action or activity

paradigm (PAR-uh-dime): a typical pattern or way of thinking

peer review (PEER ri-VYOO): a thorough look at an explanation or idea by others equally trained in that field of work

scientific inquiry (sye-uhn-TIF-ik in-KWYE-ree): the multiple ways scientists study our world

scientific law (sye-uhn-TIF-ik LAW): a mathematical equation or statement describing what nature does under a specific set of conditions

scientific method (sye-uhn-TIF-ik METH-uhd): the set of steps scientists use to conduct an experiment

Index

Websites to Visit

www.biology4kids.com/files/studies_scimethod.html

www.sciencekids.co.nz/projects/thescientificmethod.html

www.sciencebuddies.org/science-fair-projects/project_hypothesis.shtml

About the Author

Shirley Duke used her knowledge of hypotheses, theories, and laws to investigate flatworms, heartworms, ground squirrels, and grackles during her college years. Part of her fieldwork involved calling coyotes, and she can still call and get them to answer in New Mexico's Jemez Mountains. She's the author of many science books, but as a science teacher, she saw hundreds of science fair projects and the scientific method always won!

Meet The Author!
www.meetREMauthors.com

© 2015 Rourke Educational Media

www.rourkeeducationalmedia.com

PHOTO CREDITS: Cover and title page © Dimitris66, EtiAmmos; page 4 © Georgios kollidas; page 5 © pinstock; page 6, 8 © Neustockimages; page 7 © belchonock; page 9 © Peter Burnett; page 10 © Steve Byland; page 11 © Kuriputosu; page 12 © Steve Heap; page 14 © bortonia; page 15 © Proioxis; page 16 © Rich H. Legg; page 18 © Fuzz Martin; page 19 © Dizzy, Marje; page 20 © vgajic; page 21 © omgimages; page 22 © AP/Steven Hausler, AP/Nirmalendu Majumdar; page 23 © OperationsShooting, Lisa F. Young; page 24 © Desiguna; page 25 © LSkywalker; page 26 © Jordache; page 27 © The White House Historical Associaltion, LOC, Georgios Kollidas; page 29 © koya79; page 29 © LOC; page 30 © LOC, Man_Half-tube; page 31 © Alexandr Vasilyev; page 32 © Designua; page 33 © Vectomart; page 34 © Vikrom Raghuvanshi; page 36 © Alexei Crugicov; page 37 © Wellcome Library, London, oksana2010; page 39 © jut; page 41 © Leonardo Petrizi; page 43 © Johan Swanepoel, Berkeley Lab Archives; page 44 © jager

Edited by: Jill Sherman

Cover and Interior design by: Tara Raymo

Library of Congress PCN Data

Hypothesis, Theory, Law / Shirley Duke
(Let's Explore Science)
ISBN 978-1-62717-746-7 (hard cover)
ISBN 978-1-62717-868-6 (soft cover)
ISBN 978-1-62717-978-2 (e-Book)
Library of Congress Control Number: 2014935671

Also Available as: